THE BE KIND
BIBLE
STORYBOOK

A Compassion International® resource published by Tyndale House Publishers, Inc.
Visit Tyndale's website for kids at tyndale.com/kids.
Tyndale is a registered trademark of Tyndale House Publishers, Inc.
The Tyndale Kids logo is a trademark of Tyndale House Publishers, Inc.
Compassion and Compassion International® are registered trademarks of
Compassion International®, Inc.
See all Tyndale and Compassion products at www.everyoneneedscompassion.com

The Be Kind Bible Storybook: 100 Bible Stories about Kindness and Compassion.
Copyright © 2023 by International Publishing Services Pty Ltd Sydney Australia (IPS) &
North Parade Publishing Ltd Bath UK (NPP) Publishers, Peter Hicks and Wayne McKay.
All rights reserved.

Illustrations copyright © IPS & NPP. All rights reserved.
Written by Annabelle Hicks
Design consultant Jacqueline L. Nuñez
Edited by Stephanie Rische

For manufacturing information regarding this product, please call 1-855-277-9400.
For information about special discounts for bulk purchases, please contact Tyndale House
Publishers at csresponse@tyndale.com, or call 1-855-277-9400.
Library of Congress Cataloging-in-Publication Data

A catalog record for this book is available from the Library of Congress.
ISBN 978-1-4964-7872-6

Printed in China

29	28	27	26	25	24	23
7	6	5	4	3	2	1

THE BE KIND
BIBLE
STORYBOOK

100 BIBLE STORIES ABOUT
KINDNESS AND COMPASSION

Annabelle Hicks

CONTENTS

NEW TESTAMENT

Dear Parents,

God's Word tells us that others will know we are Christians by our love. And His Word gives us examples of how we can live a life of love and compassion. The 100 stories included in this Bible storybook are paired with reminders of ways we can see kindness and compassion throughout the Bible. As you read through this book, take time to discuss ways your child can show kindness to the people they come in contact with every day. It only takes one person to create change. Let it start in your home today!

Blessings,

Tyndale House Publishers
and Compassion International

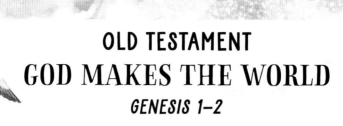

OLD TESTAMENT
GOD MAKES THE WORLD
GENESIS 1–2

In the beginning, God made light to chase away darkness. He made the sun, moon, and stars. He filled the earth with beautiful plants, the sea with amazing creatures, and the sky with colorful birds. He made animals of all kinds—huge elephants and tiny insects.

Then God made the first man, Adam, and his wife, Eve.

We can look at the marvelous things God has made and say to Him, "Thank you, God, for our wonderful world. You are so kind to us!"

ADAM AND EVE

GENESIS 2

God breathed His life into Adam and Eve. God loved Adam and Eve and gave them everything they needed. They lived in a Garden full of beautiful trees, with all sorts of plants, seeds, and fruits to eat and enjoy. Adam and Eve were kind and helped each other in the Garden.

God was pleased with everything He had made. He loved Adam and Eve and enjoyed spending time with them. He loves all people today.

ADAM AND EVE DISOBEY GOD
GENESIS 3

God told Adam and Eve not to eat the fruit of one tree in the Garden. The snake asked Eve, "Why don't you eat from that one tree? Look at its wonderful fruit! It won't hurt you!" So Adam and Eve disobeyed God. They blamed one another for their wrong choice. But God still cared for them. He gave them strong leather clothes for their life of hard work outside the Garden.

God's perfect world had been spoiled! God was sad, but He did not stop loving Adam and Eve. In His kindness, God promised to send a Savior.

NOAH BUILDS A HUGE BOAT
GENESIS 6

After many years, there were lots of people, but they were mean to one another. There was one good man named Noah who trusted God. God told Noah a Flood was coming, and he must build an enormous boat called an ark. Noah obeyed God even though many people laughed at God's warning. What God said was true: the Flood came.

Noah lived differently from his neighbors. He cared for others and listened to God, so God gave him wisdom to build the ark.

9

THE FLOOD
GENESIS 7–9

Noah's family got into the ark with two of every kind of animal on earth. Then God shut the door. It rained and rained and rained! But the ark floated safely above the water. After a long time, the ark landed on dry ground. God promised to always care for His world. God put a rainbow in the sky to remind people of His promise.

God showed compassion to Noah by saving his family from the Flood. God still shows us kindness today. Every rainbow reminds us that God cares for His world and keeps His promises.

THE TOWER OF BABEL
GENESIS 11

The people who lived after Noah were disobedient. They proudly decided to build a great, high tower! God did not want the people to think only of themselves, so He made them speak many different languages! When no one could understand his or her neighbor, they moved away and left their grand building unfinished.

The people joined together to do something selfish. God wants us to work together to love and care for others instead.

14

GOD'S PROMISE TO ABRAHAM
GENESIS 12–18, 20–21

God asked a faithful man named Abraham to go to another land. God promised to give Abraham a big family who would bring blessing to all people. Abraham trusted God and obeyed. Abraham waited a long time with no children at all—but he still believed God. At last, the promised son was born to Abraham's wife, Sarah. They called the baby Isaac.

God's promise came true. Abraham's children had many children— and many years later, Jesus came into that family, bringing blessing to the whole world and to us today.

16

GOD HELPS FOOLISH LOT

GENESIS 13, 18–19

Abraham said to his nephew, Lot, "You choose where you want to live." Lot chose a valley that looked good—but the people there were wicked. Abraham was worried and prayed to God. God kindly sent an angel to rescue Lot and his family.

Even though Lot had made a foolish choice, God knew that he did not follow the wicked ways of people around him. God lovingly sent help to Lot's family.

A HAPPY WEDDING
GENESIS 24

Abraham wanted his son Isaac to marry a lovely woman who would follow God's ways. A servant traveled a long way to where Abraham used to live and asked God that the right girl would offer him water from the well. Soon God brought beautiful Rebecca to the well! When Rebecca and Isaac met, they fell in love and got married!

God wants to guide us in the big and little choices in our lives. He is all-wise, and His way is always the best one!

TWIN BOYS
GENESIS 25, 27–28

Isaac and Rebecca had twin boys: Esau and Jacob. One day, when Esau was very hungry, Jacob convinced Esau to trade him the firstborn family privileges for a bowl of stew!

When Isaac was old and nearly blind, Jacob cheated to get his father's special blessing. Jacob dressed up as his brother by making his smooth skin feel hairy. His lie worked, and he got the blessing. Esau was angry, so Jacob ran away.

God took care of Jacob, even though he made a wrong choice. God never stops loving us.

A VERY SPECIAL DREAM
GENESIS 28

Jacob dreamed of a stairway reaching heaven with angels going up and down. God gave him big promises: "I am the Lord God. I will watch over you and be with you and bring you back to this land." Jacob learned that God is great and kind. Now Jacob wanted to follow God's way.

God's love and kindness changed Jacob's heart. Instead of taking from other people, he promised to give part of all he had to God.

A FAMILY OF TWELVE BOYS
GENESIS 37

Jacob had a favorite son, Joseph, and gave him a multicolored robe. Jacob's other sons were jealous and angry—made worse when Joseph dreamed that his brothers' bundles of corn bowed to his bundle; and the sun, moon, and stars bowed to him.

The brothers sold Joseph to become a servant in Egypt and smeared his robe with blood. Heartbroken Jacob believed Joseph had been killed.

God lovingly watched over Joseph. God saw faith and honesty in Joseph's heart. The dreams were actually a peek into God's good plan.

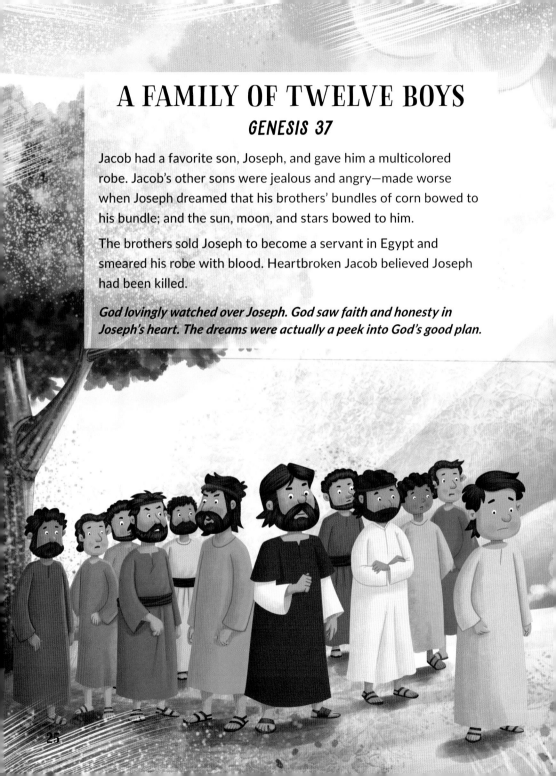

A KING'S DREAMS

GENESIS 41

Pharaoh was worried by his dreams: seven thin cows ate up seven fat ones; then seven thin heads of grain ate up seven fat ones! God showed Joseph that this meant seven years of huge harvests before seven bad years. Joseph's new job as a leader was to store up grain throughout Egypt in the years of plenty.

Joseph had a special job in God's big plan. Abraham's great grandchildren would not die of hunger but would number as many as the stars!

MOVING TO EGYPT
GENESIS 42–47

The seven years without much food began. People from far away came to Egypt to buy food—including Joseph's brothers. The brothers bowed to the Egyptian ruler, not knowing it was Joseph! Joseph's dreams had come true! Joseph learned that his brothers' wicked hearts had changed. With tears of joy, Joseph hugged them and arranged for them all to move to Egypt.

Joseph's brothers had done nothing to earn Joseph's kindness, but Joseph was kind anyway. God helps us follow Joseph's example of forgiving those who hurt us.

MOSES—A BABY IN A BASKET
EXODUS 1–3

A new pharaoh made God's people, the Israelites, work hard and said, "No more baby boys!" One mother hid her baby boy in a basket by the river—and the king's daughter found him. The baby's name was Moses. When he grew up, Moses wanted people in Egypt to be treated fairly, but some were slaves. God told Moses, "I will rescue My people. Tell Pharaoh to set them free."

In His goodness, God gave Moses an important job. God saw that His people were suffering, and He chose Moses to help them.

TERRIBLE TROUBLES
EXODUS 7–12

Moses spoke God's words to Pharaoh, but Pharaoh said, "No!"

God sent bad river water, frogs, gnats, flies, sick animals, sores, hail and fire, locusts, and three days of darkness. Pharaoh still said, "No! I will not let your people go!"

The last terrible trouble was coming: the oldest boys would die. But the oldest boys were safe if a lamb died instead. Now Pharaoh saw how powerful God is. Pharaoh said, "Yes!"

The oldest boys were safe when a lamb took their place. Jesus is the Lamb who died in our place. We can depend on Him to care for us.

34

A PATH THROUGH THE SEA
EXODUS 14

The Israelites marched out of Egypt! But Pharaoh changed his mind. Now Pharaoh's army was behind the Israelites, and the Red Sea was ahead of them. Moses trusted God to help. God made a path through the sea, and the Israelites all crossed safely. When the Egyptians tried to follow, they got stuck and the water collapsed around them.

God miraculously made a way for the freed Israelites to give them a great future. God's love is with us always—on miracle days and ordinary days!

36

FOOD IN THE DESERT
EXODUS 15–16

The Israelites moaned and complained in the hot desert, not knowing where to find food or water. They even wished to go back to Egypt! They stopped praising God for freeing them from Pharaoh—but every morning God cared for them by providing amazing food. They called the food manna, which means "What is it?"

Jesus taught us to ask our heavenly Father for our "daily bread" because God has not changed. He still loves to provide for His children.

GOD'S COMMANDMENTS
EXODUS 20

God offered the people blessings and peace and joy. If they chose to honor God and obey His commands, they would be able to enjoy God's loving presence. Some of these commands include "respect and obey your parents" and "do not lie." God always loves us and wants us near Him. We show God that we love Him by obeying His commands.

Jesus said that God's rules can be summed up like this: "Make God first in your heart and love other people as you love yourself."

41

MOSES PRAYS
EXODUS 33

More than once, the Israelites stubbornly broke their promise to obey God. Now the people would go ahead to their new land, but God would not be with them. Moses begged God to forgive and guide them. God knew the people could not live without Him, and His kind heart answered, "Yes. I will be with you."

Moses was amazed by God's compassion and forgiveness. Every single moment God is totally holy, and every single moment God is totally compassionate.

42

THE TWELVE SCOUTS
NUMBERS 13–14

Moses sent twelve men to explore the promised land of Canaan. Carrying back delicious fruits, ten reported, "The land is full of milk and honey, just as God promised—but there are strong people and big cities! We cannot go there!"

Only two men trusted God and said, "Let's go at once! God is with us!"

God loves us enough to let us make choices. Let's remember His wonderful love and care and choose to trust Him—rather than our own strength.

THE BRONZE SNAKE
NUMBERS 21

The Israelites forgot God's kindness and began to complain against Him. God was grieved and angry that the people did not trust Him. But the people soon repented when poisonous snakes came into their camp. They were afraid, but Moses prayed to God for them. God instructed Moses, "Make a snake and put it on a pole. Anyone who is bitten can look at it and live."

God hears our prayers and is kind to us. He heals those in need. This story is a symbol of Jesus on the cross. Anyone who looks in faith to Jesus gains forgiveness and eternal life.

JOSHUA BECOMES THE LEADER
DEUTERONOMY 29–31

Old Moses encouraged the people to remember God's goodness: "God always wants the best for you, but you must choose! If you follow God's way, He will watch over you. If you live selfishly, you will lose your land and find life is hard." Moses handed his job over to Joshua, "You are now the leader. Be strong. God is with you!"

God did not make rules to spoil life—but so that people could live in the very best way possible and enjoy all God's blessings.

48

THE PROMISED LAND

JOSHUA 1–6

God made a path through a river, and Joshua led the Israelites into the Promised Land! Ahead was the city of Jericho. For six days, the Israelite army marched around its huge walls, and they marched around the city seven times on the seventh day. Trumpets sounded and Joshua commanded, "Shout! God has given you the city!" God made the walls tumble down!

God had kept His promises: Abraham's family grew into a huge crowd and arrived in the land God had promised them! We can always trust what God says.

GOD CHOOSES GIDEON

JUDGES 6–7

Many years passed. Enemies kept taking the Israelites' crops and animals. At last, the Israelites asked God for help. God sent Gideon to lead them. One night, Gideon's men silently circled the enemy camp with hidden torches. Suddenly, they broke their jars, lifted their torches, and shouted! The enemies were surprised and afraid—and ran away! God helped Gideon win with three hundred soldiers against thousands!

Gideon learned it is better to trust God than to depend on people. God is waiting to hear our requests—so let's not forget to ask for His guidance.

RUTH MEETS BOAZ
RUTH 1–4

Naomi was a woman who loved God. Her husband and sons died, but her daughter-in-law Ruth promised to always live with her. Naomi and Ruth moved to a new country and needed food. Boaz, a kind farmer, deliberately left grain for Ruth to collect in his field and shared his lunch with her. When Boaz married Ruth, Naomi knew that God had arranged this great joy.

Boaz gave to Ruth and Naomi when they were in need. God blessed Boaz's kindness. Many years later, Jesus was born into Boaz and Ruth's family to bless the world.

GOD HEARS AND ANSWERS HANNAH

1 SAMUEL 1–3

Hannah longed for a child and promised God, "If You give me a son, I will let him work for You." God said, "Yes!" Hannah was so thankful that she sang a song about God's amazing love! Her little boy, Samuel, grew up in a place of worship and learned to listen for God's voice.

Hannah was thrilled at God's generous compassion for her. God filled her life with more children to love and enjoy.

DAVID, THE SHEPHERD BOY
1 SAMUEL 16

When Samuel was an adult, God sent him to anoint a king from a certain family. Seven boys were tall and handsome, but God said, "No! I am not looking at appearances, but at their hearts." Finally, the youngest, David, came in from looking after his sheep—he was the one God had chosen! David wanted to worship God with all his heart.

God is always looking inside our hearts! When we worship Him first, everything else will find its right place in our lives.

DAVID FIGHTS A GIANT
1 SAMUEL 17

Israel's enemies had a champion. David visited his frightened soldier brothers just as the enemy giant shouted, "Send one man to fight me!" David said, "God has saved me before from a bear and a lion. I trust God to help me win!" David hurled one stone, the giant fell to the ground, and the enemies scattered!

God saw the Israelites being treated badly by their enemies. Because David loved and trusted God, God chose David to lead His people.

DAVID IS KIND
2 SAMUEL 9

King Saul hated David, but the king's son, Jonathan, was David's best friend! When David became king, he wanted to show kindness to Saul's family because of Jonathan. David met Saul's grandson, Mephibosheth, who was unable to walk. David restored Mephibosheth's family land to him and invited him to always eat at the palace.

God loves all people and wants us to be kind. We can ask God to help us see and love the people around us.

THE SHEPHERD SONG BY DAVID
PSALM 23

The Lord is my Shepherd,
so I have everything I need!
I can rest in green meadows
near clean, refreshing water.
He teaches me how to honor His name.
I am not afraid in the dark valley,
because He is with me
always keeping me safe.
I will live with Him forever!

David wrote many beautiful songs. In the Shepherd Psalm, David described God as the wonderful Good Shepherd, always caring and providing for us, His sheep.

GOD IS MERCIFUL
PSALM 51

God, please be merciful
because of Your great compassion.
Wash away all my wrongs and make me clean.
I am wrong, and You are right.
Give me a pure heart that's strong to follow You.
Please don't take Your Holy Spirit from me.
Give me joy as I praise You.
I know You are looking for humility.

David learned that God is right to be angry with sin, but God is merciful and never turns away anyone who has a humble, sorry heart.

GOD IS GREAT

PSALM 103

Never forget how kind and forgiving God is!
He fills us with energy!
He does not stay angry and has not punished us as we deserve.
Measure from east to west—
that's how far He has taken our sins away!
Like a father, He understands us completely.
The Lord is King over all. Praise Him, my soul!

David was so thrilled with God's amazing love and forgiveness that he called all the angels and all creation to join him in praising God!

GOD NEVER SLEEPS
PSALM 121

I look at strong mountains—but my help does not come from there!

My help comes from the Maker of heaven and earth.

He never sleeps, and He is watching over me.

The sun won't harm me by day, nor the moon by night.

The Lord is always watching to keep me secure!

God made us, loves us, and wants us to stay close to Him under His protection—day and night.

70

A SPECIAL GIFT FOR SOLOMON
1 KINGS 3; 2 CHRONICLES 1

God asked David's son, "What shall I give you, Solomon?"

Solomon answered humbly, "I want to be a good king. Please give me wisdom to rule Your people. Show me what is right and what is wrong."

God was pleased and said, "Yes! Follow in My ways, and I will also give you riches and a long life."

God longs for us to walk in ways He can bless. When we ask, God gives us wisdom to know right from wrong and strength to choose the right path.

THE MAGNIFICENT TEMPLE
1 KINGS 5–8; 2 CHRONICLES 2–7

After seven years, thousands of workers finished building a magnificent Temple with huge stones, special wood, lots of gold, and wonderful fabrics. They placed special objects for worship inside. King Solomon prayed, "God, You created everything and do not live in buildings, but here we want to be close to You and hear Your Word."

God says to us, as He did to Solomon, "Yes! I will be with you." God lives in people. We can worship God wherever we are!

ELIJAH AND THE RAVENS
1 KINGS 17

Generations later, King Ahab and Queen Jezebel worshiped made-up gods called idols, so God warned, "For two years there will be no rain." Without rain, the crops didn't grow.

Ravens brought bread and meat to God's prophet, Elijah. Later, God sent Elijah to help a widow and her son. They had hardly any food. Elijah said, "Make bread for me, and God will provide more!" And that's what happened!

After every loaf was made, there was always flour and oil for the next time! God loves to give generously, especially when we are ready to share with others.

WHO IS THE TRUE GOD?
1 KINGS 18

Elijah organized a contest. Jezebel's idol worshipers set up a sacrifice. All day, hundreds of them begged their god to send fire. Nothing happened! Then Elijah repaired God's altar with twelve stones, topped with wood and the sacrifice. Elijah soaked the altar with water and prayed, "Please show these people that You are God!" God's fire burned up everything—even the stones!

God is the only true God! He is all-powerful and deserves our worship. He listens when we pray to Him.

NAAMAN IS HEALED
2 KINGS 2, 5

After Elijah went to heaven, a new prophet named Elisha took his place. Elisha spoke God's words too. Naaman, an important Syrian soldier, had a skin disease. A little girl working in Naaman's house told Naaman that God would heal him. Naaman traveled far to see Elisha in Israel, who said, "Dip in the Jordan River seven times." Naaman did not think that was a very good idea—but eventually he obeyed what God had said through Elisha—and God completely healed him!

It was a little girl who cared for Naaman and shared the good news of how God would heal him. Who can you encourage with good news today?

JOASH, THE BOY KING
2 KINGS 11–12; 2 CHRONICLES 24

The king of Israel died, and the king's family argued about who would be the next ruler. Baby Prince Joash was secretly rescued and hidden in the Temple. When Joash was seven, he was crowned king instead of his wicked family members. King Joash trusted God and led many people back to following God's rules, even though they would disobey again.

Joash became king when he was a child. God loves everyone: adults, teenagers, and young children! No one is too young to be part of God's plan.

ISAIAH, GOD'S HELPER
2 KINGS 17; ISAIAH 6

A man called Isaiah saw a vision of God sitting on a high throne surrounded by angels. God's holiness filled the room, and Isaiah felt how sinful he was. God saw Isaiah and forgave his sins. When God asked for a volunteer messenger, Isaiah answered, "Send me!"

Isaiah preached, "God loves you. Turn back to Him." The people refused to listen. Strong enemies marched in and took their northern kingdom.

Although God is holy, He loves us and wants us to be near Him. He calls to us, with open arms and the offer of forgiveness!

GOOD KING HEZEKIAH
2 KINGS 18–20; 2 CHRONICLES 29–32

King Hezekiah ruled the southern kingdom. He restored the Temple and called his people to worship God. God forgave all who truly wanted to follow Him.

Strong invaders, camped nearby, boasted that no god could stop them. Hezekiah asked God to rescue His people and show His power. That night, God's angel defeated the enemy! Hezekiah's soldiers did not have to fight!

God cares, listens, and answers! Hezekiah's heart was upright, and Hezekiah wanted God's name to be honored. God answered Hezekiah's prayers and rescued His people.

JOSIAH AND THE LOST BOOK
2 KINGS 22–23; 2 CHRONICLES 34

Years after Hezekiah was king, eight-year-old Josiah became king. He wanted to bring people back to God's ways. During his reign, temple workmen found the neglected, dusty "Book of God's Law." Josiah read it and was distressed that people had forgotten God's standards. When God's commandments were read out loud, everyone promised to turn back to God and get rid of the idols.

Everything changed when people listened to God's Word! His Word is always true and up-to-date. It teaches us how to follow God.

A LESSON IN THE POTTER'S WORKSHOP

JEREMIAH 18, 29

Jeremiah was a man with a message from God. He preached, "God has good plans for you! You are like misshapen clay that the potter can remake into a new pot. God can make you new! But if you will not change and follow Him, enemies will come and take your land."

God's heart overflowed with love and good plans for His stubborn people—but they would not listen. We must choose: Do we follow God's way or our own?

DANIEL'S THREE FRIENDS
DANIEL 3

Daniel and his friends were Israelites taken from their home. In Babylon, King Nebuchadnezzar ordered everyone to worship his huge golden idol—or be punished. Daniel's three friends said, "No! We only bow to God." Nothing could harm them because God's angel was protecting them. They were pushed into a hot fire—but it did not even burn their clothes! The king learned there's only one true God.

God is King over all the rulers in the world. If rulers make laws against God's commands, we must choose to obey God. His way is always the best way.

DANIEL AND THE LIONS' DEN
DANIEL 6

Jealous men plotted against Daniel. They knew he prayed to God.

So they flattered the king, "Majesty! Make a new law! People must only pray to you—or be thrown in with lions!"

Daniel did not stop praying. He was forced into a cave with hungry lions. God's angel protected him and shut the lions' mouths! The next morning, Daniel walked out unharmed!

Daniel knew God and trusted Him totally. In His kindness, God watched over Daniel and protected him from the evil men's plans.

RETURNING TO JERUSALEM
EZRA 1–3; HAGGAI 2; ZECHARIAH 8

God's promise was coming true! The Jewish exiles returned home with recovered treasures raided years earlier from God's Temple.

After the long, tiring journey, the travelers cried! Their beautiful city was ruined, and the Temple was a heap of rubble. As they rebuilt, God's messengers encouraged them, "Remember, God is with you!"

When we are tired and sad, we can remember that our loving God is with us. He always keeps His promises!

BUILDING THE WALLS OF JERUSALEM

NEHEMIAH 1–10

Far from home, Nehemiah, a leader of the Israelites, received news: "Jerusalem's walls are ruined." His generous employer sent him home with building materials! Nehemiah got everyone working; some built and others watched for enemies. The huge walls were finished in fifty-two days! When God's rules were read aloud, the people realized they had failed, and they promised to obey.

Nehemiah organized the people to work together as one big team. With God's strength, we can work together with family and friends to help our communities.

A BEAUTIFUL QUEEN
ESTHER 1–7

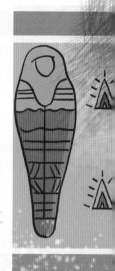

The Persian king loved his Jewish queen, Esther. Proud Prime Minister Haman loved praise—but Esther's cousin would not bow to him. Haman tricked the king into signing a law to kill all Jewish people: "Majesty! Jewish people disobey your laws. Punish them!" The king didn't know they were Esther's people. Esther bravely told the king that Haman's plan would kill her. The angry king punished Haman instead.

Esther bravely spoke up when she learned about Haman's wicked plan. God blessed her courage and watched over the Jewish people.

JONAH AND A GREAT FISH
JONAH 1–3

Jonah was a prophet chosen to speak God's words. But he disobeyed God's instruction to preach in Nineveh. Jonah did not want God to forgive those people. He boarded a ship going the opposite way, but the ship met a dreadful storm. It was Jonah's fault, so he was thrown into the sea. God sent a huge fish to swallow him and, three days later, to spit him out! After that he obeyed God.

All people in every country around the world are made by God, and God cares equally for each one. We can help bring God's message of forgiveness and compassion to all people.

NEW TESTAMENT
THE SAVIOR IS COMING
LUKE 1; MATTHEW 1:18–25

An angel visited a woman named Mary and told her that through God's power she would have a baby boy—Jesus, the Savior of the world! An angel visited Joseph, Mary's soon-to-be husband, too. He was glad to take care of Mary and her baby.

God's big plan was unfolding! God loved the world so much that He would send His Son from heaven into the world to be the Savior!

JESUS IS BORN
LUKE 2

Joseph and Mary had to travel to Bethlehem. But there was no room for them to stay in an inn. Mary's baby, Jesus, was born and was cradled in a manger. Shepherds were first to hear the news from an angel: "Today the Savior has been born. He is in a manger!" An angel choir sang, "Glory to God! Peace on earth!" The shepherds rushed into Bethlehem and found that it was true!

God chose ordinary shepherds to be the first to meet and worship Jesus. The shepherds excitedly told everyone they knew that the Savior had been born!

FOLLOWING A STAR
MATTHEW 2

Wise men were following a star. They knew a King had been born. At King Herod's palace they asked, "Where is the new King?" Jerusalem was the wrong place! They set off for Bethlehem, and the star led them to where Jesus was. They worshiped the child and gave Him gold, frankincense, and myrrh.

Jesus would be a different kind of ruler than King Herod. Herod just wanted power, but Jesus would show that He is a King who is good and kind.

JESUS IS BAPTIZED
MATTHEW 3; MARK 1; LUKE 3; JOHN 1

John was a bold man who lived in the wilderness and preached, "Be truly sorry. Turn from your sins. Welcome God's Kingdom, and be baptized!"

As Jesus approached, John announced, "Here is the Lamb of God!"

God's Spirit rested on Jesus, and God called out, "You are My Son, and I love You!"

John said, "I'm only using water to baptize—but Jesus will pour out God's Spirit!"

Because God loved the whole world, He sent His Son as the Lamb of God to take the punishment for our sins and give us new life in Him.

JESUS IS TESTED IN THE DESERT
MATTHEW 4; MARK 1; LUKE 4

After forty days in the dry, hot desert, Jesus was very hungry. The devil said, "If You are God's Son, turn stones into bread!" He was trying to trick Jesus. But Jesus answered, "People need more than bread in their stomachs. They must also hear God's words." Two more times, the devil tempted Jesus to follow a selfish path—but Jesus never did.

Jesus perfectly showed us what God is like and how to live God's way. He loved God completely and loved others perfectly. He knew that God would take care of Him and was never selfish.

112

JESUS TURNS WATER INTO WINE

JOHN 2

Jesus' mother was worried! Mary, Jesus, and His followers were guests at a wedding party where the wine had run out! Jesus told the servers to fill large jugs with water and take the jugs to the head waiter. The head waiter was amazed: "This is the best wine—which people usually serve first!" he said.

Jesus saw His mother's worry and felt compassion for her. He gave her what she needed. Just like Jesus turned the water into wine, He helps us change from the inside out.

AN EVENING WITH NICODEMUS
JOHN 3

Nicodemus was a teacher who wanted to learn from Jesus. Jesus told Nicodemus, "Unless a person is born again, he cannot see God's Kingdom. Just as you were born into your human family, you need to belong to God's family! God loved the world so much that He sent Jesus, so that everyone who believes in Him will have eternal life."

We can't make up our own ideas of how to join God's family—we must come God's way! God invites everyone to believe in Jesus.

A THIRSTY WOMAN
JOHN 4

Jesus rested by a well. A woman came with her bucket. Jesus asked her for a drink and said, "I can satisfy your spirit with living water like a fountain. My water gives life that never ends!"

After they talked, the woman ran to the villagers. She said, "I've met someone who knows everything about my life! I think He's the promised Savior!"

Jesus knew the woman had broken many of His rules, but He showed her kindness. He offered her a fresh start with God's Spirit inside her. The woman could not wait to share this good news!

JESUS VISITS NAZARETH
LUKE 4

Jesus visited the place of worship in his childhood town of Nazareth. He read out loud from God's Book, "God's Spirit is with Me to preach good news to the poor, to announce freedom for prisoners, to give sight to the blind, to release those who are burdened, and to proclaim this is the time of God's blessing!"

The words Jesus read aloud were about Himself, although they had been written hundreds of years earlier. Jesus came to help and heal!

120

JESUS THE HEALER IN CANA
JOHN 4

A child near Cana was dying, and his father—an important official—begged Jesus to come and heal him. Jesus said, "Go home—your son will live!" The man believed. He arrived home to find that the fever had left the boy at the exact time Jesus had spoken. All the official's household became believers in Jesus.

While He was on earth, Jesus showed compassion to many people and healed all kinds of illness. Jesus still hears everyone who calls to Him in faith.

121

SICK PEOPLE AROUND A POOL
JOHN 5

Many sick people lay around a pool, believing that when the waters stirred, the first person to get in the pool would be healed. One man had been sick for thirty-eight years.

Jesus instructed him, "Get up, pick up your mat, and walk!" And he did!

Some people were angry that Jesus healed someone on the day of rest, but Jesus cares more about people than traditions.

The sick man did not think he would ever be healed. But Jesus saw him and made him well. God wants us to see the needs of the people around us and help them.

JESUS THE HEALER IN GALILEE
MATTHEW 4; MARK 1; LUKE 4–5

A man with a dreadful skin disease kneeled and begged Jesus, "If You are willing, I know You can heal me." Jesus touched the man and said, "Of course! Be healed!" Immediately, the disease went away.

Everyone wanted to be near Jesus! Jesus could not enter a town quietly, so crowds came to Him out in the countryside.

The man with the skin disease was used to being treated as an outcast. Filled with compassion, Jesus touched Him when no one else would. Jesus' touch healed Him!

FOUR FRIENDS ON A ROOF
MARK 2; LUKE 5

Four men carried their paralyzed friend but couldn't get near Jesus, so they lowered him through a hole in the flat roof! Jesus said, "Friend, your sins are forgiven." Some people thought, *Only God can say that!* But Jesus is God! He forgives and heals. Jesus told the paralyzed man to stand up and go home—and he did!

Jesus had compassion on sick people as well as those suffering from sin. He freely healed people's bodies, forgave their wrong choices, and still takes care of us today.

TRUE HAPPINESS
MATTHEW 5–7; LUKE 6, 12

Jesus taught, "Truly happy people are humble, gentle, and kind. They want to do what is right and bring peace.

Love your enemies, and do good to them!
Do for others what you would like them to do for you.
Think about your own faults before judging others!
Ask God for what you need. He loves to give good gifts."

As God's children, we will never find happiness in wanting money or lots of things. Instead, we will find it when we put God first and treat others well.

A LESSON FROM BIRDS AND FLOWERS

MATTHEW 6; LUKE 12

Jesus said, "Don't long for lots of money and things—they won't last, and they take all your attention. Collect treasures in heaven!

Don't worry about clothes, food—or anything! Learn from the birds in the sky. God feeds them! Since He cares for birds and dresses flowers so beautifully, He will surely take care of you!"

God has compassion and good plans for everyone and everything in His wonderful world. He wants us to trust Him and copy His love and kindness.

133

HOW TO PRAY
MATTHEW 6; LUKE 11

Jesus taught His followers to talk to God like this:

"Our Father in heaven,
We pray that people will respect Your name.
We long for Your Kingdom and Your will.
Give us the food we need each day.
Forgive us our sins, as we forgive others.
You are King with power and glory forever,
Amen."

*We need God's forgiveness—but we also need to forgive
others. God can help us to show grace, like He does.*

134

A WISE PERSON
MATTHEW 7; LUKE 6

Jesus said, "Everyone who puts My teaching into practice is like a wise man building his house on rock. That house will stand against the storm!

But if you hear My words and take no notice, you are like a foolish man building his house on sand. His house will completely collapse in the storm."

Jesus spoke words of eternal life. It's important for us to build our lives according to Jesus' words, hearing and obeying what Jesus said!

JESUS TELLS A STORY: THE FARMER'S SEED
MATTHEW 13; MARK 4; LUKE 8

A farmer scattered his seed. Seeds that fell on the path were immediately eaten by birds. Seeds that fell among rocks began growing but soon withered because their roots had no soil. Seeds that landed among thorns became choked. But the seeds that landed on good soil grew into a great crop.

To grow in God's Kingdom, we must say no to worrying and wanting possessions. We are like the tall, healthy crops when we are fully committed to God's way.

JESUS CALMS A STORM
MATTHEW 8; MARK 3; LUKE 8

Jesus had chosen twelve men to be His disciples. One evening, they were all in a boat together. Jesus fell asleep. A sudden strong storm began. The disciples panicked, shouting, "Jesus! Help! We're going to drown!"

Jesus replied, "Why are you afraid? Your faith is small!" He stood up and ordered the wind and waves to be quiet. Immediately, the sea was peaceful!

Jesus saw His disciples' scared faces and had compassion on them. He stopped the storm and reminded His disciples to trust Him.

JESUS RAISES A LITTLE GIRL FROM THE DEAD
MATTHEW 9; MARK 5; LUKE 8

A father named Jairus begged Jesus to come and heal his dying little girl. Then a messenger brought news that the girl had already died. Jesus said, "Don't fear; only believe." Outside the house, Jesus ordered, "Stop the noise and crying! She is not dead, but asleep."

Inside, Jesus held the girl's hand and said, "Child, get up!" And she did!

Jesus is stronger than death. When Jairus's family felt hopeless, Jesus showed that they could hope in Him.

A HUGE PICNIC
MATTHEW 14; MARK 6; LUKE 9; JOHN 6

After a long, busy day helping crowds of people, Jesus' followers said, "Send everyone home!"

Jesus cared that the hungry people had to walk a long way home. "No," said Jesus. "They need food!"

Jesus multiplied five small loaves and two little fish. He made more than enough food to feed over five thousand people!

Jesus cares about the everyday needs of tired, hungry people! In His kindness, He fed the whole crowd instead of sending them away hungry.

JESUS LOVES CHILDREN
MATTHEW 18; MARK 10; LUKE 18

Jesus always had time for young children! Someone asked, "Who is the greatest in God's Kingdom?" Jesus answered, "Anyone who welcomes a little child, welcomes Me. To enter God's Kingdom, children and grown-ups need the simple faith and humility of a child. Humble people who trust God are the greatest in the Kingdom."

Being humble means following Jesus' example and looking for ways to serve others instead of ourselves. Jesus says humble faith will be blessed!

JESUS TELLS A STORY: A GOOD NEIGHBOR

LUKE 10

Robbers attacked a traveler, stole all his things, and left him at the roadside. Two Temple workers ignored the hurt man as he lay in the dirt. But a man from a hated people-group had great compassion. He bandaged him, put him on his animal, paid for him to stay at an inn, and took care of him overnight.

That man went out of his way to be a good neighbor!

Caring for others is not always easy. Sometimes it takes time or money, or we would rather do something else. But God commands us to be kind and to love others as God loves them.

JESUS TELLS STORIES:
A LOST SHEEP AND A MISSING COIN
LUKE 15

If a shepherd has one hundred sheep and one gets lost, he goes out to search for it. Returning home with the sheep on his shoulders, he calls to his friends, "Rejoice! I have found my lost sheep."

Or imagine a woman who loses one of her ten silver coins. When she searches and finds it, she is so happy!

The shepherd and the woman did not give up searching until what was lost became found. In the same way, God cares about people who are far from Him. There is great joy in heaven when they come back!

JESUS TELLS A STORY: THE LOVING FATHER

LUKE 15

A boy wanted his freedom! He took money from his father, set off—and soon wasted everything. He got a job feeding pigs and was so hungry he wished he could eat their food! He decided to go home and say sorry. His father saw him coming and ran to meet him with a great, big welcome.

God is always ready to forgive us and welcome us back home. Our sins are never bigger than His compassion for us.

JESUS TELLS A STORY:
TWO MEN IN THE TEMPLE
LUKE 18

Two men went to the Temple to pray.

The proud man celebrated himself, announcing, "I'm glad I'm not like bad people—I do good and give away money!"

The humble man prayed, "God, please have mercy. I know I am a sinner!"

God heard and forgave the second man.

The proud man was not talking to God but to himself so that others would hear and think highly of him. God hears our prayers when we are humble and sorry and depend on His kindness.

THE RICH RULER
MATTHEW 19; MARK 10; LUKE 18

A rich man asked Jesus, "How can I inherit eternal life?"

The man said he had kept all God's rules. Jesus loved him and said, "Sell your belongings, give everything away to the poor, and you will have treasure in heaven. Then follow Me."

The rich man was sad because he loved his earthly treasures. He turned and went away.

The rich man loved his possessions more than he loved God. When we make God first in our hearts, He has promised to care for our needs.

A NOISY BLIND MAN
MATTHEW 20; MARK 10; LUKE 18

A blind man learned that Jesus was coming. He would not stop shouting, "Jesus, Messiah, have pity on me!"

Jesus stopped and asked him, "What do you want Me to do?"

The blind man replied, "Lord, I want to see!"

Jesus responded, "Receive your sight! Your faith has healed you."

Instantly, the man could see!

Jesus often cared for people one at a time. He could have hurried by the blind man, but instead He stopped, spent time with the man, and healed him. Is there someone you can help today?

A MAN UP A TREE
LUKE 19

A rich man, Zacchaeus, wanted to see Jesus—but he was short and there was a crowd. He ran ahead and hid up a tree! Jesus stopped, called him down, and visited his house.

In front of everyone, Zacchaeus told Jesus, "Lord, I'm giving half my fortune to the poor. If I have cheated anyone, I'll pay back four times the amount!"

When Zacchaeus met Jesus, his heart was completely changed. He wanted to fix what he had done wrong. When we harm someone else, God wants us to ask for forgiveness and make it right.

EXPENSIVE PERFUME
MATTHEW 26; MARK 14

At a supper with friends, a woman gave something precious to Jesus. She poured out a valuable jar of beautiful perfume over His feet.

Some jealous people grumbled, "That perfume was worth a lot of money that could have been given to the poor!"

Jesus said, "No! She did something beautiful."

The woman loved Jesus more than anything and wanted to give Him something special. How can you find a way to say "I love you" to Jesus today?

163

HOSANNA!

MATTHEW 21; MARK 11; LUKE 19; JOHN 12

Jerusalem was full of visitors for a festival. Jesus was coming too! As Jesus rode into the city on a young donkey, people ran ahead laying down branches and their cloaks. Children danced as they praised Him! Crowds were waving branches, cheering, and shouting, "Hosanna! Blessed is the One who comes in the name of the Lord!"

Jesus rode into the city as the King, and He deserves all worship. He came with power to save all people who trust in Him from the punishment of their sins.

164

TROUBLE IN THE TEMPLE
MATTHEW 21; MARK 11; LUKE 19

The Temple courts were filled with noisy stalls for worshipers to buy animals for sacrifices and to exchange money. Traders made money unfairly from those who had traveled far.

Jesus was angry! He threw out the greedy traders and overturned their tables, saying, "My house will be a place of prayer for all nations, but you are making it a den of thieves!"

God does not like it when people behave unfairly. God wants us to copy Jesus by following what is right, treating others with kindness, and living humbly before God.

A WIDOW'S GREAT GIFT

MARK 12; LUKE 21

Jesus told His disciples, "I watched rich people put lots of money into the Temple offering box. But do you see that poor widow? She only put in two little coins—but she gave more than everyone else! They put in some of their spare money, but she gave all that she had to live on."

Jesus is always looking at our hearts! Measured by their own standards, the rich people felt proud. But Jesus saw that the widow gave generously out of her love for God.

JESUS WASHES FEET
JOHN 13

Jesus and His friends were sharing a celebration meal. After supper, Jesus took off His cloak and wrapped a towel around Himself, just like a servant. He poured water into a bowl, washed each of the disciples' feet, and dried them.

Jesus said to His disciples, "Follow My example: serve one another as I have done."

Washing someone's feet is a dirty job! Jesus did it to teach His disciples how to treat others with extravagant kindness. Jesus commands us to follow His example.

REMEMBER JESUS
MATTHEW 26; MARK 14; LUKE 22

Jesus would soon leave His friends. After they ate their meal, He handed some bread around and said, "Eat bread together and remember Me."

Jesus took a cup of wine, thanked God, and passed it around for them all to share. He told them, "I am going to die to bring forgiveness. When You drink this, remember Me."

Jesus gave us Communion—a simple way to remember His sacrifice. There is no greater love than the love God has for us!

172

JESUS DIES ON THE CROSS
MATTHEW 27; MARK 14–15; LUKE 22–23; JOHN 18–19

The religious leaders had studied hard to become teachers. They were jealous when Jesus so clearly explained things about His Father, God. They made up false stories and sent soldiers to arrest Jesus.

Cruel soldiers hurt Jesus and nailed Him to a cross. Jesus asked God to forgive them. Then Jesus died. But soon He would be alive again!

God allowed cruel men to put Jesus on the cross. Jesus loved us and gave His life for us so that we can be forgiven!

JESUS IS ALIVE

MATTHEW 28; MARK 16; LUKE 24; JOHN 20

Followers of Jesus gently buried His body in a garden cave on Friday evening. Very early on Sunday morning, some women went there to visit and remember Jesus.

Then came great excitement! The cave was empty, and an angel announced, "Jesus is not here—He has risen! Hurry and tell His followers!"

At any time of year, we can celebrate Jesus' triumphant victory! Jesus has risen; death is defeated! Now, anyone who believes in Jesus can live with Him forever.

A STRANGER ALONG THE ROAD
MARK 16; LUKE 24

Two sad friends talked together as they walked home with a stranger, saying, "We believed that Jesus was the promised Savior, but He was cruelly killed. Incredibly, some are saying the burial cave is empty and He is alive!"

The stranger explained that those things were always in God's plan. Suddenly, they realized the stranger was Jesus. He really was alive!

God's plan was always for Jesus to die and rise again. When we believe in Jesus, He gives us new life. We can share the Good News with others!

IT'S REALLY JESUS
MARK 16; LUKE 24; JOHN 20

The friends rushed to Jesus' followers and were excitedly telling their news when Jesus Himself came into the room. The followers weren't sure if He was real, so He said, "Touch Me—I have flesh and bones! Do you have anything I can eat?" With joy and amazement, they watched Him eat fish and heard Him explain how God's plan had come true.

Jesus appeared to His followers in large and small groups over a period of forty days. There was no doubt that He was truly alive again!

BREAKFAST ON THE BEACH
JOHN 21

Seven disciples went fishing at night but caught nothing. At sunrise, Jesus was on the beach calling, "Throw your nets on the right-hand side, and you will catch plenty!" They obeyed and could hardly haul in the net full of 153 large fish!

"Come for breakfast," Jesus invited them. He had bread ready and a fire ablaze to cook the fish .

Jesus understood the feelings of the tired, disappointed fishermen. With Jesus' miraculous help, the fishermen's sadness turned to joy!

THE BEGINNING OF THE CHURCH
MATTHEW 28; MARK 16; LUKE 24; ACTS 1–2

Jesus instructed His followers, "Teach people everywhere to obey My words. The Holy Spirit is coming to help you." After Jesus had gone back to heaven, the Holy Spirit came, sounding like rushing wind and appearing like flames! Peter boldly preached to a crowd. Thousands of people asked God for forgiveness. The church had begun!

The church is not a building, but it is the people who trust in Jesus and have God's Holy Spirit. The Holy Spirit gives us power to do what is right, comforts us when we are sad, and changes our hearts to love God and others more and more.

TALKING ABOUT JESUS
ACTS 3

A man who could not walk sat begging as two of Jesus' followers, Peter and John, approached the Temple.

"I don't have any money," Peter said, "but I can give you something better! In the name of Jesus Christ of Nazareth, I command you to get up and walk!"

The man stood up and started walking, then began jumping and praising God!

Peter and John healed the man with power from God's Spirit. God is happy when we care for the needs of others.

ON THE ROAD TO DAMASCUS

ACTS 9

Saul wanted to stop everyone who followed and worshiped Jesus. One day, a bright light from heaven blinded him and a voice called, "Saul, why are you hurting Me?"

Saul asked, "Who are You, Lord?"

The voice replied, "I am Jesus. I have chosen you to preach for Me."

Saul had news to tell: "I met Jesus! Jesus is God's Son!"

When God's Spirit came into Saul, everything was changed! Saul was given a brand-new goal: to share the news of Jesus. Later he would be given a new name: Paul.

BARNABAS IS A GOOD FRIEND
ACTS 9

The Christians were amazed and a little scared of Saul because he had been their enemy. A friend called Barnabas brought Saul to the Christians and reassured them, "Saul really is a Christian now. I have heard him preaching that Jesus is God's Son!"

Barnabas and Saul traveled far together, helping people and telling them about Jesus.

Barnabas welcomed Saul and stood up for him. He was a loyal friend to Saul and many others. God's Spirit helped Barnabas to be kind and generous.

GOOD NEWS FOR EVERYONE
ACTS 10

A Roman centurion, Cornelius, called his family and friends together to hear Peter preaching, "God has no favorites! He loves people of all nations! Jesus came from God, and we saw His miracles. He died on a cross, but God raised Him—we saw Him alive! When you believe in Him, you have forgiveness of your sins."

Cornelius and his household believed in Jesus! They were from a different country than Peter. But God's kindness extends to all people in the world!

PAUL AND BARNABAS GO TRAVELING

ACTS 13–15

Saul, who was now called Paul, and Barnabas traveled from town to town preaching forgiveness through Jesus. Those who believed started churches. When Paul and Barnabas healed a man, people thought they were gods. Paul explained there is only one true God. Some people welcomed the news about Jesus—but some hated the missionaries and their message!

God loves all people, but only some people decide to love God back. We can pray for people who do not love God—that they will change their minds and choose to trust Him.

194

PAUL AND SILAS GO TRAVELING
ACTS 16

In Jesus' name, Paul and another missionary, Silas, set free a girl who was treated unkindly. Her angry masters started a riot, which landed Paul and Silas in prison. At midnight, as Paul and Silas sang hymns, an earthquake shook the doors of the prison open!

Paul shouted to the jailer, "Don't worry! No prisoners have escaped!" Later, Paul explained God's love and forgiveness, and the jailer's family became Christians.

Paul and Silas could have complained about their problems, but instead they remembered God's goodness and started singing! When the doors flew open, Paul and Silas did not choose to escape. Their kindness and God's power led the jailer to trust in Jesus.

TIMOTHY THE TRAINEE
ACTS 16; 2 TIMOTHY 1

Ever since Timothy was a child, Timothy's mother and grandmother taught him God's Word. Timothy showed that he was trustworthy. Paul treated him like a son, training him and Silas to be preachers. Timothy became a caring leader and a good example to everyone in the churches.

Praise God for everyone who teaches God's ways! We should surround ourselves with trustworthy people who love God and will encourage us to live rightly before Him.

PAUL TRAVELS TO ROME
ACTS 27–28; ROMANS 8

Paul's preaching trips took him to grand cities and little villages. In many communities a church was started. Much later, Paul made his final boat trip toward Rome—and that journey included experiencing a shipwreck! An angel told Paul that God would bring everyone safely to dry land—and that's what happened. Paul never stopped sharing the good news of Jesus.

Paul wrote to encourage the new churches, "God is always kind to us—nothing can harm us. Nothing can ever separate us from His great love!"

OUR WONDERFUL HOME
JOHN 14; REVELATION 21–22

Jesus is preparing a place for His followers to live with Him forever. There's a clear flowing river and the tree of life with marvelous fruit. Light is everywhere, and the doors are always open. There is nothing impure or unkind—no tears, no pain, no darkness, no need for the sun or moon. Best of all, we will see Jesus and be at home with Him!

God has always loved us and wants us to be close to Him. He wants to share His home with us forever!